# FACT CAT

# AMPHIBIANS

Izzi Howell

## FACT CAT

Get your paws on this fantastic new mega-series from Wayland!

Join our Fact Cat on a journey of fun learning about every subject under the sun!

Published in paperback in 2017 by Wayland
Copyright © Hodder and Stoughton 2017

ISBN:  978 1 5263 0039 3
Dewey Number: 597.8-dc23
10 9 8 7 6 5 4 3 2 1

MIX
Paper from responsible sources
FSC® C104740

Wayland
An imprint of Hachette Children's Group
Part of Hodder & Stoughton
Carmelite House
50 Victoria Embankment
London EC4Y 0DZ

An Hachette UK Company
www.hachette.co.uk
www.hachettechildrens.co.uk

A catalogue for this title is available from the British Library
Printed and bound in China

Produced for Wayland by
White-Thomson Publishing Ltd
www.wtpub.co.uk

Editor: Izzi Howell
Design: Clare Nicholas
Fact Cat illustrations: Shutterstock/Julien Troneur
Other illustrations: Stefan Chabluk
Consultant: Kate Ruttle

Picture and illustration credits:
Corbis: Fabio Liverani/Nature Picture Library 14, Stephen Dalton/Minden Pictures 15, Ch'ien Lee/Minden Pictures 17b; iStock: ABDESIGN 4tl, WitR 4bl, EcoPic 5, kerkla 7, MikeLane45 8l, nicolasprimola 9, Mark Kostich 10, pok-ergecko 12, Franang 13t, kikkerdirk 13b, WitR 17t, Karon Troup 18t, Mark Kostich 18b, AndreyTTL 20; Shutterstock: worldswildlifewonders cover, Birute Vijeikiene title page and 16, groveb 4tr, Jason Patrick Ross 4br, Ryan M. Bolton 6, Matteo photos 8r, jacglad 11, reptiles4all 19, Dr. Morley Read 21l and 21r.

Every effort has been made to clear copyright.
Should there be any inadvertent omission,
please apply to the publisher for rectification.

The author, Izzi Howell, is a writer and editor specialising in children's educational publishing.

The consultant, Kate Ruttle, is a literacy expert and SENCO, and teaches in Suffolk.

## FACT CAT FACT

There is a question for you to answer on each spread in this book. You can check your answers on page 24.

# CONTENTS

# WHAT IS AN AMPHIBIAN?

Amphibians are a group of animals that are similar to each other in certain ways. Almost all amphibians start their lives in water. They move on to land when they are adults.

Frogs, toads, newts and salamanders are all examples of amphibians. What's the difference between a frog and a toad?

poison dart frog

American toad

smooth newt

red salamander

Some amphibians make noises to let other amphibians know that they are nearby. Frogs and toads blow air into parts of their throats to make a croaking sound.

Bullfrogs have a low, loud croak. Some people think that it sounds like a cow mooing.

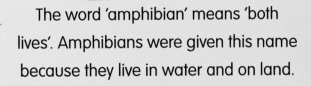

FACT CAT FACT

The word 'amphibian' means 'both lives'. Amphibians were given this name because they live in water and on land.

# HABITAT

Amphibians live in warm **habitats** because they are **cold-blooded**. Cold-blooded animals can't control the temperature of their bodies. They are warm if they are in a hot place, and cool if they are in a cold place.

Spotted salamanders stay in the shade, under leaves and logs, so that they don't get too hot.

**FACT CAT FACT**

Some amphibians change the colour of their skin as the weather changes! They become darker when it's cold and lighter when it's hot. This helps them to stay at the right temperature.

All amphibians need to keep their skin **moist**, so they live in **damp** areas near lakes and rivers. Most adult amphibians, such as toads, live on land. However, some adult amphibians, such as newts, spend most of their time in water.

Red-eyed tree frogs live in the rainforests of South America. How do the feet of a red-eyed tree frog help them to climb up trees?

# YOUNG

Most amphibian **larvae** (young) hatch from soft eggs. **Female** amphibians usually lay their eggs in lakes or rivers because larvae can only breathe underwater.

FACT CAT FACT

Cane toads can lay up to 350,000 eggs in one year!

Toads lay their eggs in long strings.

Frog eggs are laid close together. What is another name for frog eggs?

The larvae of some amphibians, such as frogs, look very different to adults. Their bodies slowly change during the stages of their life.

This drawing shows the different stages in a frog's life. Over time, tadpoles (frog larvae) lose their tails and grow legs.

# BREATHING

Amphibian larvae can breathe underwater through their **gills**. As they grow into adults, skin covers their gills and they breathe air with their **lungs** instead.

This eastern newt has lungs. It has come to the **surface** to breathe air.

Most amphibians can breathe through their skin if it is wet. To keep their skin moist, amphibians must live in a damp habitat.

The common toad can breathe through its skin, as well as with its lungs.

FACT CAT FACT

Adult lungless salamanders can only breathe through their skin. When they become adults, they lose their gills, but never grow lungs.

# SKIN

Some amphibians hide from **predators** by being in a habitat that is the same colour as their skin. This is called **camouflage**.

The grey tree frog can change the colour of its skin to match the colour of the tree that it is sitting on.

FACT CAT **FACT**

The skin of amphibians is so thin that water can pass through it. This means that amphibians don't need to drink water.

Some amphibians have brightly coloured skin. The bright colours let predators know that these amphibians are **poisonous**, so that they don't eat them.

When a fire salamander is in danger, it squirts a poisonous liquid all over its body.

Just one golden poison dart frog has enough poison to kill twenty humans! How long is a golden poison dart frog?

# DIET

Most amphibians begin their lives as **herbivores**. Larvae eat water plants and **algae**. As adults, many amphibians are **carnivores**. They catch worms and insects on land, and they hunt small fish in water.

FACT CAT FACT

Ornate horned frogs close their eyes to help them swallow large **prey**. Closing their eyes helps to push food into their stomach.

This edible frog is eating a dragonfly.

cricket

Frogs and toads hunt by quickly wrapping their long sticky tongues around their prey. They pull their tongues back into their mouths to eat what they have caught.

This White's tree frog is about to catch a cricket with its tongue. Is a frog's tongue joined to the front or the back of its mouth?

# MOVEMENT

Adult frogs use their strong, long back legs to jump forward quickly. Toads have shorter back legs than frogs. They move by crawling or by making small jumps.

Frogs are excellent swimmers. They use their **webbed** feet to push water backwards and their body forwards.

FACT CAT FACT

Some frogs can jump more than 20 times the length of their body in one leap!

Adult newts and salamanders have four short legs and a tail. They can't jump, but they can walk on land and swim in water. Caecilians (si-sil-yuns) don't have legs or a tail. They live underground and use their pointed heads to dig through the soil.

A newt has a flat tail which helps it to swim through water.

Caecilians look like snakes, but they are amphibians because their skin needs to stay moist. What type of animal is a snake?

# SENSES

Most amphibians use their good eyesight to hunt for food. Amphibians that live underground, or in **murky** water, use their sense of smell to find prey, because it is difficult for them to see.

Mole salamanders can see very clearly in the dark. This helps them to catch prey during the night.

FACT CAT **FACT**

Amphibians have an extra set of eyelids that protect their eyes underwater or while they are sleeping! Which other animals have an extra pair of eyelids?

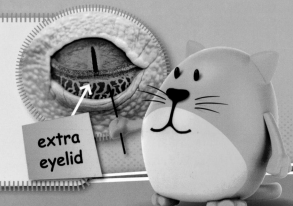

extra eyelid

Hearing is important for amphibians. Frogs and toads **communicate** with each other with croaking noises. They also need to be able to hear if a predator is nearby.

ear

A frog hears with large circular ears on the side of its head.

# STRANGE AMPHIBIANS

Axolotls (axe-a-lot-als) are a type of salamander that can breathe underwater, even as an adult. This is because axolotls don't lose their gills. Axolotls spend their whole lives in water.

**FACT CAT FACT**

If an axolotl loses a leg, it can grow another one in its place!

Some people keep axolotls as pets. Which country do axolotls come from?

Glass frogs live in trees in the rainforests of South America. They were given their name because the underneath of their bodies is see-through, just like glass!

If you look carefully underneath this glass frog, you can see its stomach and heart.

A glass frog from above

Try to answer the questions below. Look back through the book to help you. Check your answers on page 24.

**1** Amphibians are warm-blooded. True or not true?

a) true

b) not true

**2** Which amphibian lays its eggs in long strings?

a) salamander

b) frog

c) toad

**3** Some amphibians have brightly coloured skin to show predators that they are poisonous. True or not true?

a) true

b) not true

**4** Which adult amphibian has a tail?

a) frog

b) newt

c) toad

**5** Amphibians that live underground use their sense of smell to find food. True or not true?

a) true

b) not true

**6** Where do glass frogs live?

a) in trees

b) in the desert

c) in lakes

# GLOSSARY

**algae** a plant-like living thing without a stem or leaves

**camouflage** a way of hiding by being the same colour as the area you are in

**carnivore** an animal that only eats meat

**cold-blooded** describes an animal whose body temperature depends on the temperature of their surroundings

**communicate** to share information by making noise

**damp** describes something that is slightly wet

**female** describes an amphibian that can lay eggs, from which young will hatch

**gill** a part of the body that some amphibians breathe through

**habitat** the area where a plant or an animal lives

**herbivore** an animal that only eats plants

**larva** a young, growing amphibian that has hatched out of its egg

**lung** a part of the body that is used for breathing

**moist** describes something that is slightly wet

**murky** describes something that is dark and not easy to see through

**poisonous** describes something that can hurt or kill you if you eat or touch it

**predator** an animal that kills and eats other animals

**prey** an animal that is killed and eaten by other animals

**surface** the top part of something

**webbed** describes toes or fingers that are joined together by skin

# INDEX

# ANSWERS

## Pages 4–21

**Page 4:** Frogs have moist skin and move by jumping. Toads have drier skin and move by crawling. Frogs spend more time in water than toads.

**Page 7:** Their feet have suction pads which stick to the tree and stop them from falling off.

**Page 8:** Frogspawn

**Page 13:** 2.5 centimetres

**Page 15:** The back of its mouth. This means that its tongue can reach things that are far away from its mouth.

**Page 17:** Reptile

**Page 18:** Some animals include dogs, sharks and eagles.

**Page 20:** Mexico

## Quiz answers

1  not true – they are cold-blooded.

2  c - toad

3  true

4  b - newt

5  true

6  a – in trees